1

# RETIREMENT

## Early plan best result.

Graeme Smith

PUBLISHED ON AMAZON.com
by
LABYRINTH BOOKS

## DEDICATION:

**This book is dedicated to my family.**

**Hele-ly (Ly).**
    my wife:

**Ingrid.**
    our daughter:

**Marie.**
    my former wife:

**Fiona, Natalie and Michael**
    our children:

**Georgie**
    Michael's wife:

**Pearl, Kiki and Martha.**
    their children:


They have had to put up with me for many years and I thank them for that.
I hope this book gives them an insight into what has occupied me.
All have done worthwhile and interesting things in the absence of my help.
I congratulate them for their achievements.

## SUPPORT:

The International Artist magazine – international magazine for artists

The Australian Artist magazine – magazine for artists

Clipping Path Universe – for photo-shop editing

Cherri Computers – for computer hardware, software and printers

# HOW TO USE THIS BOOK.

**First think - then do.**
Usually people don't think through things to the level they need to.
Because of that, they have projects instead of tasks on their "to do" list.
That leads to procrastination as it hasn't been broken down to a task level.

**So go through your book once to understand it.**
Go through it again.

**Then start at the idea you would like to implement first.**
Make notes of the steps you will need to take and the resources required.
Use these notes to create a step by step system for implementing the guide.
Often you will not refer to the original, once you've created **YOUR** system.

**The first question to ask and answer is "Why is this being done?"**
How does this align with where you want to get to?
What are the strategic implications of doing this?
Does this fit with getting to your goal in the shortest and fastest time?
What would it be like if it were totally successful?
Define it - what is success for this project and how will you know?

**Now brainstorm all the tasks that are involved in your project.**
It's important not to go linear too fast with this.
By linear, I mean step one, step two, step three, and step four.
You end up cutting off options.
As you plan step one, two, three, there is a specific step that might be four.
Start steps too quickly, other ways for one, two and three may not appear.

**The first third of any brainstorming session is really easy.**
Just come up with lots of ideas.
The second third is challenging - go through ideas and see where they lead.
Then push yourself to think a little bit outside the box.
That's often where the big idea is!
That's where the most powerful way of getting a project done fastest - is.

**Most people never get to that level and short-change themselves.**
Then their project takes longer and they also set up to procrastinate.
This final brainstorming part of the equation is incredibly important.

**Once fully brainstormed put your options into a linear sequence.**
Then you can figure out what you've overlooked.
Everything becomes obvious as you get your tasks in order.
Now add missing steps and you have laid out your task list for this project.

**When you've organized the tasks into a linear process decide:**
What things can you start immediately?
What can be started that are not dependent on what occurred before them?
Obviously that is step one.
There might be step five, six or twenty that don't rely on anything else to do.
You can get started on them right away too.

**Now use a folder.**
Write things you think of at the time and also cross off things as you do them.
Add in stuff that is relevant from time to time.

## Index: RETIREMENT.

**SUPPORT:**
Cherri Computers – for computer hardware, software and printers

The International Artist magazine – international magazine for artists

The Australian Artist magazine – magazine for Australian artists

Clipping Path Universe – for photo-shop editing

# 1. Why Retire?

Reviewed by Mark Kingston - (Sydney, Australia)
1. Most artists I know don't want to retire.
2. But can you retire?
3. The start stops most people.


## 1. Most artists I know don't want to retire.

**They want to keep painting until they go to the big studio in the sky.**
But sometimes circumstances make this impossible.
You have an accident, debilitating ill health, or no-one want to buy your stuff.
Money must come from somewhere or it's very difficult to live these days.
This doesn't just apply to the aged, but then is more difficult to cope with.
But there is actually something you can do, that most other people can't.
Provided people still want to buy your paintings you can do it yourself.
Set up a superannuation scheme **BUT** you **MUST** maintain a sales presence.

**Some years ago I talked to one of my gallery's artists about this.**
He mentioned advice he had years before from a Sydney gallery-owner.
My artist was advised to keep all unsold works from any exhibition.
The Sydney gallery owner told him to put them away and forget about them.
For in his old age these paintings would be very valuable.
They are the only ones from early periods of his career and are sought after.
People and institutions look for works like these to fill holes in collections.

**The Sydney gallery owner talked to a successful professional artist.**
Unsold works by the artist would be of a similar standard to those sold.
Otherwise they would not have been exhibited at all.
The gallery owner didn't suggest inferior unsold works as superannuation.
Inferior works should not be exhibited, let alone kept for the future.

**The late Fred Williams is reputed to have had a similar idea.**
It's said, every second painting Fred did was put away in a shed.
The others were exhibited, sold and dealt with in the usual fashion.
Those in the shed were Fred's superannuation.
If the story is true, he has left a magnificent legacy to his family.
They can sell a few each year, and live quite comfortably.

**Fred died many years ago and I believe this has been the case.**
**BUT even if it's not, it still illustrates what's possible.**

**Another prominent Australian artist is Brett Whitely.**
I'm not sure if he put works away for the future or they just accumulated.
Never-the-less many of Whitely's paintings were in his estate.
Court cases about this legacy only serve to illustrate its value.

**A few years ago we exhibited Judy Cassab's work.**
Judy was 75 years old and seemed in good health but say she was infirm.
Paintings available from earlier in her career could still be exhibited and sold.
Many people are keen to buy an artist's work at this stage in their life.
So there's often a demand for work by elderly artists that cannot be met.
If you've kept sufficient works for this eventuality, then it's possible to cash in.
This could be for your own benefit or for relatives and other beneficiaries.

**The artists are Australian but undoubtedly other artists do the same.**
Obviously the younger you are when you put the works away the better.
Fred Williams was not that old when he died, and neither was Brett Whitely.
Be systematic and you can retire in the future if you wish, or must.

**Superannuation is about putting something aside for your old age.**
In recent years governments encourage people to control their retirement.
They want people to be in superannuation schemes.
They've even forced employers to provide superannuation for employees.
Government approaches to superannuation are heavy handed and complex.
They are not particularly suited to the needs of artists.
Can your superannuation be included in the government's current definition?
The law is complex so these notes are based on an assumption you can't.
But be guided by your accountant on this, not me.

**There are likely to be taxation aspects to be considered.**
However even taking this into account, you'll still have advantages.
Particularly when compared to most other people, in looking after your future.
Declare these works as part of your trading stock.
You'll be required to pay tax on their value at the time they are declared.
The value can be cost of production (paint, paper, canvas, frame and so on).

**I believe this is probably what your accountant would advise you to do.**
The works are part of trading stock so are not subject to capital gains tax.
In these circumstances you'll not have to pay capital gains tax, years later.
That's when the works are sold, given away, or even bequeathed.

**A variation on the above involves work by other artists.**
You can buy other people's work, or exchange with your artist friends.
There are traps if you broaden your superannuation collection this way.

## 2. But can you really retire?

**The other day some friends were talking about planning for retirement.**
They were trying to figure out what they could do to retire earlier.
Maybe you've been through this exercise too but more likely you haven't!
You may be disenchanted, ill, die or cease to be a professional artist.
You may stop painting or reduce activity to an occasional past-time.

**Few artists even consider retirement – but they should!**
Professional artists may eventually want to retire or have no choice.
If they think at all about it likely to be hope they can paint until the last breath.
However retirement **IS** something worth thinking about.
You can then live in a garret in poverty or have the lifestyle you'd like.
Early planning of retirement can lead to a very pleasant lifestyle.

**It doesn't necessarily mean you have to stop painting though.**
It's more likely you stop having to earn money by painting.
That's where you started - you painted for fun, satisfaction and pleasure.
If you have enough income then you can do it again if you want to.
You can give up painting completely as it's your choice after you retire.

**How about early retirement?**
This isn't forced retirement but early retirement where you have a choice.
You might not want to retire as an artist and even fancy dying at the easel.
**BUT** if you can retire, whether you do so or not, there are some advantages.
But the first thing to do is to start early, and that means to-day.
There is no earlier time than that to begin the retirement process!
You need to budget wisely and maintain financial discipline.
This doesn't necessarily mean saving money, although you can do that.
But investing in growth assets rather than lifestyle (cars, holidays).

**You MUST have a budget AND you need cash-flow now!**
Without spare money you can't do much.
Basically you will have very limited choices.
In retirement your financial situation should not depend on artwork sales.
Do you want to paint until your last breath to keep bread on the table?
Not much of a life is it?
But if you retire early you can still paint because that's what you chose to do.

**If you start early enough you can build a retirement income source.**
**BUT** be realistic about your lifestyle and also what you can achieve later.
Invest at a level of risk you are comfortable with (if everything goes wrong).

**Contrary to much advice don't diversify but concentrate the risk.**
Best to invest in what you know and understand than something you don't.
You can diversify later if you wish when your capital base has been secured.

## 3. The start stops most people.

**Back in my art student days I learnt this lesson.**
It's been a lesson that has stayed with me through my life.
I often express it a little differently but let me tell you my (true) story.
I was in the third year of a four-year art course.
Our lecturer for one class didn't have much to say when he was there.
But often he wasn't there, or late, or went early, or a combination of those.
Frequently he was even a little inebriated.
My fellow class members followed his pattern as it was a night class.

**One memorable evening I arrived for class to find I was the only one!**
I decided not to waste my time.
I had driven an hour and a half through peak hour traffic to be there.
I looked at my blank canvas and didn't know what to do.
I was reasonably successful and nearly three quarters through the course.
**BUT** I did not know what to do for the start certainly had me stopped.
Have you had this feeling - it was totally unexpected.
I now realize that teachers and lecturers provide the starting point.
One is not usually put in the situation that I found myself.

**After a while, I looked at my paints and noticed a tube of Indian Red.**
I decided that I'd use that, as it is a colour I dislike.
If I was going to waste some paint it may as well be a colour like that.
I still didn't know what to do though.
I mixed the Indian red with some turps, with no real thought about what to do.
Then just because the paint was runny, I flicked some onto the canvas.
I splashed some more.
Still further splashes followed the first ones.
I looked at the canvas for a while, all covered with splashes of Indian red.
It was a bit like an Indian red 'Jackson Pollock'.
Still not knowing what to do, I decided to join up the dots.
After a while, I looked again at the canvas, all covered with irregular shapes.

**But I was no further ahead in working out what to do.**
More speculation led me to the idea that I could colour some of the shapes.
This I did.
I squeezed out white and made shapes with this and Indian red mixtures.
I was quite busy doing this.
Eventually I finished and had another look at what I had done.
Even though I didn't know what to do, I had done something.
It was an abstract painting to be sure.
I was pleased with the result, even though not anticipated before starting.

**The next week the same thing happened.**
Instead of splashing paint, I shut my eyes and made random marks.
I don't remember whether I used Indian red, probably not I think.
Anyhow again I developed an abstract painting.
I continued like this for the rest of the year.
I even took this newfound attitude into other classes.
Teachers and lecturers provided starting points, even of a realistic nature.
But no longer did the start stop me.
I had found out the solution to that particular artistic problem.

**It doesn't matter what you do at the start, as long as you do something.**
It can even be quite random like my first couple of self-discovered starts.
BUT that doesn't necessarily have to be the case.
Have you ever waited for inspiration?
Did you find that you had to wait for a long time?
There is no need to wait just make a few marks on the paper or canvas.
That's what your mind needs to feed on.
Imagination cannot work on a blank surface, it needs help!
So whenever you feel artist's block, just do something, anything.

**This lesson actually applies to anything at all!**
The hardest part of any task is starting.
Once you start there is some momentum and you can now gather pace.
Most of the energy required for a car or rocket is used right at the start.
But once things are moving it is easy to keep going.
We are **NO** different.

**The hardest part of retiring is starting.**
There is a tendency to put it off!
It's just not urgent.
Just do what I did (not necessarily with Indian red or even splashes).
Do anything that will get you moving towards retirement.
It doesn't have to be a big step for any step at all will do.

**As time goes by you can modify and change what you did at first.**
This is how Bill Gates started Microsoft!
In a similar fashion your retirement plan will improve too.
By the time you actually retire you may have a Rolls Royce retirement plan.
BUT if you do not start you never will have any kind of retirement.

## 2. Manage change.

Reviewed by Alison Murphy - (Brisbane, Australia)
1. To retire you will need to change what you do in some way.
2. A transition strategy from career to retirement is required.
3. Some key traits needed for a successfully managed retirement.
4. In retirement, scale down rather than completely cease sales.

### 1. To retire you will need to change what you do in some way.

**Write down your answers to questions like these:**
What have you achieved?
Why was this so?
What has changed?
What things would you like to keep?
Which are the main problem areas?
Add answers to other questions that arise.
The sooner this is done the better.

**Now you have a base for developing an appropriate retirement plan.**
But to do this you'll need to write down answers to questions like:
How many years will it be until I want to retire?
Where do I want to be in five years with my career retirement?
How much money would I like to be making then?
How much will I need in retirement?

**Write down all the steps you need to take in order to move from:**
Where you are now (first notes).
To where you'd like to be in five years (second notes).
Make each step quite small and therefore achievable.
Do this as soon as possible and now you are ready to move!
Implementation of your plan should coincide with the start of a quieter period.
Then focus on that without being too distracted by day-to-day requirements.
Carry out your retirement plan, already developed, so it becomes a reality.
The changes you want do actually start to happen.

**It's the most important and difficult, phase and requires full attention.**
That's why it's better if you can commence in your quieter period.
But if this isn't possible, then start rather than delay.
It's always better to do something rather than nothing.
What about monitoring change too?
As you implement your retirement plan you'll find parts need changing.
This happens, so make changes rather than locking in earlier decisions.

**This changing process will only improve your retirement plan.**
Change is on-going so there's not really any point in delaying.
There will never be a better time than right now, to start towards retirement.
That applies even if you are at the very beginning of your career!

## 2. A transition strategy from career to retirement is required.

### It can be a scary time for many people so they put off retirement.
They wait for the right time, which never comes!
There is no right time, other than when you say let's do it now.
But you are ready to wind down your career sot how are you going to do it?
Perhaps you keep doing what you have been just spend less time?
Will that get you there and how can you be sure?
Well maybe you'll do what you see other artists doing instead?
But you're likely to obtain similar results (at best) to those they attain.

### On the other hand look at your new career phase as a challenge.
This is probably the better way, for it surely will be.
Just what is the challenge that confronts you?
It's not just to conclude a professional art career is it?
The real challenge is to be able to continue to live well.
What this means will only be if you make it happen which takes planning.

### Initially strategic (long term) planning is required.
You have to know where exactly you want to get to in (say) five years.
In that period of time someone else can become a Ph. D.
You need the same qualities of character as a university graduate.
I'll mention some of these shortly, they are totally dedicated to their objective.
Can you have that kind of commitment to achieving your goals?

### The best thing to do is to decide where you'd like to be in five year's.
Imagine in the future and you are looking back on the past five years.
What did you achieve, what can you do now you couldn't when you began?
Make a list of all those things BUT be specific.
Just saying you are retired is not enough - that's just a dream.

### How much will your annual income be (then)?
How many works do you sell and what kind of works are they?
What are their prices (on average) and what sorts of people buy your work?
Where do you sell them - through galleries or elsewhere - which galleries?
How busy are you - are you getting the idea?

### Now this isn't what is happening now is it?
What exactly do you need to do to achieve those future retirement goals?
Write down what you have to do and your goals will guide your thinking.
Do whatever is necessary to head in that direction.
Don't begin things that take you away from that they waste precious time.
There's a great deal of thought and planning required.

**OK what do you do first?**
Sit down and think carefully.
Gallery representation is key to retirement and too important to muck up!
Moving from where you are now to where you'd like to be is continuous.

### 3. Some key traits needed for a successfully managed retirement.

**Perseverance and persistence:**
Without this nothing will happen.
You've probably heard that 'faint heart never won fair lady';
Well your retirement will not happen either unless you stick at it too.
Staying power keeps you going when times get tough is absolutely essential.
There will be tough times.
This quality can even make up for deficiencies in other areas.

**You must believe in yourself.**
Feel you can overcome obstacles and barriers or give up at the first hurdle.
Without self-confidence you'll always be shackled by doubts.
Enthusiasm provides the drive necessary to overcome those hurdles.
You'll also visualize a greater number of opportunities that you can tackle.
It also generates a positive attitude that attracts people to your cause.

**You must believe in the worth of being a retired professional artist.**
Often people don't really believe it is a worthwhile thing to do.
What you believe influences thoughts, actions and outcomes of your plans.
Luck never goes astray too.
But luck is a willingness to discern opportunities and take advantage of them.
It's closely linked to optimism.

**Being concerned is different from worrying.**
Concern is a realistic understanding that problems are likely.
Concern lets you prepare for challenges before they become significant.
Sometimes it's important to be able to change direction.
Unexpected opportunities may arise and if not taken will be lost forever.

**One the other hand sometime things do not work out as expected.**
Not always do we attempt things at the most opportune time.
You need to adjust and try again, or put aside an action for the moment.
Problems are not failures but temporary setbacks from which we can learn.
This thinking means you can deal with the next setback that is inevitable.
Particularly if you analyze what happens and learn from the experience.

## 4. In retirement, scale down rather than completely cease sales.

### It's money in your bank account that is your major concern.
So cost price should be the focus of your sales.
It doesn't matter if one person sells your work and make more than another.
As long as sales take place and you get the amounts you want - important.
Monitor the selling prices by all means.
A variety of sizes gives an idea about the effectiveness of your retail outlets.
If works are selling readily you might consider an increase in wholesale price.

### For many artists, pricing is their single biggest worry.
Will pricing in retirement be any different?
They also hear a great deal of advice; much of it quite misguided.
In retirement you may be tempted to think only of securing immediate sales.
But you should still go about it in a logical fashion.

### Usually artists price according to the size of their works.
Without going into the reasons you should continue this in retirement.
It keeps your price structure consistent with the past.
Avoid making your best works in your smallest sizes.
Reduce the number of larger works as they take longer to do.
Gradually increase the price of all works.

### The best people to ask for advice are your potential customers!
Have a small function, and invite a number of potential buyers (10 or 12).
Have some eats and drinks and show them some of your works.
Select typical works in the range of sizes that will be retirement income.
Tell the people you want to do market research to help you get things right.
Ask them to write down what they think these works would sell for.
Also ask would they be likely to buy works such as these.
Ask how much they'd pay (which could be different).
Ask any other questions you want answers to.
Collect the answers, and then have a general discussion.

# 3. Do you still need clients?

Reviewed by Terry Horn – (Johannesburg, South Africa)
1. Can you maintain a part-time art career?
2. Are you now in a business or do you have a hobby?
3. Which clients make your career in retirement?
4. It's really great when someone is referred by a previous buyer.

## 1. Can you maintain a part-time art career?

**Bring in other people to form a team to manage your career transition.**
Letting go of your baby is not an easy thing to do - particularly at first.
Most of us are bits of loners as far as our art is concerned.

**Ask for and accept outside advice from proven competent advisors.**
An outsider will almost certainly have skills you need and are lacking.
Accounting, marketing, legal or whatever that person brings to your table.
They will see things you don't!

**Appoint a business advisor a person with business ability you respect.**
Someone outside your immediate family with relevant business background.
Not your accountant or lawyer as they already have their roles.
Their opinion unbiased, objective, independent, and without excess baggage.

**Pay for performance and pay the market rate.**
Then people gain a feeling of self-worth.
Rather than merely doing a bit of this and a bit of that!
Their rewards are not ad-hoc.
Have job specifications and a salary structure for everyone.
Specific job descriptions for everyone including yourself and family members.
Make sure you use the best person for any job.

**Decide entry and exit criteria.**
Have ground rules as well as an induction and an exit program.
They are based on what is best for your career and retirement.
These rules should apply to family members as well as the outside advisors.
They should not be based on your relationship with individuals.
Everyone in your business gets a fair and impartial go.

**Distribute information and communicate.**
An artist is traditionally very secretive about his/her business.
Your career and retirement vision is communicated to all in your business.

## 2. Are you now in a business or do you have a hobby?

**If you are still doing any works you'll probably want to sell them.**
It won't matter whether you are a scaled back professional or a hobby artist.

**BUT you can't do both.**
Well at least according to the taxation department of your country.
There are likely to be different rules depending on which you are.
You probably know about those differences.

**In retirement you may mainly paint for pleasure or even not at all.**
Thus you are a hobby artist even if your accountant suggests otherwise.
That doesn't mean you will not continue to sell works.
**BUT** certainly not in the quantity that you did before retirement.

**Talk to an accountant and find out your position on taxation laws.**
Otherwise you haven't really retired.
You need to make sure of levels of income you can earn, in your situation.
Do that before you start declaring that income and expenses as well.
You may need to limit sales so that you don't go over the income threshold.
You don't want to join the business people once more.

**So it's still a good idea to maintain records of income and expenses.**
Then you'll be able to keep track of the financial cost of your hobby.
And be in a position to take best advantage of a switch to the business ranks.

**In retirement you will be doing less.**
That's the point of retirement.
An attempt to please everyone is the biggest single mistake you could make.
There will always be people who want something different from what you do.
That's also why you need to be careful when you listen to people.
Do they want something different and are steering you in that direction?
If so, be polite but take no notice.

**It's better to decide what you do and get on with it.**
Don't worry at all about those who want something different.
Decide what you really want to do and focus on that.
Also decide how much of it you want to do.

**If you have a narrow focus you can still be one of the specialists.**
You can still be competitive on a reduced output.
In retirement the idea of specializing is very strong so focus according to your interests and skill.

## 3. Which clients make your career in retirement?

**When you retire you'll be on your own.**
Even in retirement you'll still need clients if you need income.
Then it is too late then to build a contact list so start to-day.
No sales = no money = no career of any kind!

**In retirement you want fewer clients but NOT none.**
How many depends on projected output **BUT** best are those you have.
They know and trust you because they have dealt with you previously.
You are not a stranger to your past clients.
Provided you treated them well in the past they're likely to stick with you now.
Start collecting their names, addresses and phone numbers, now.

**This may take quite a while to start with so start early – like NOW.**
As time goes by it gets easier, for many of the names are repeated.
And you know where they are and you know what they buy.
So they will provide the best return on an investment of time and money.
Both are key aspects of your retirement.

**Because you update regularly you'll develop a qualified list.**
Qualified means it has been sorted and is appropriate for its intended use.
The list comprises people who bought or are interested in buying your work.
You can then contact these people whenever you wish.
You can tell them about the forthcoming retirement for example.

**Often the address will not be complete.**
It's a name and suburb but even so, put this information in your list.
Do detective work to find out the remaining information when it's needed.
It's important to have listed people who are interested in buying your work.
They are more difficult to identify but many come in casual conversations.
Make sure you get name and address before the conversation is forgotten.

**There are many different offers you can make.**
These range from special discounts, to opportunities to buy before other
clients, invitations to special functions, to get to meet you, and so on.
Your imagination is the only limit to the range of offers you can construct.

**Some people are big users of a product or service.**
Some don't make much use of it at all are other artists good clients?
Some people are easy to sell to and spend up big.
Others are always causing more work for you and spend the least.

**About 20% of your clients generate 80% of your turnover.**
This statistic is true in all businesses and is known as the 80/20 rule.
Obviously the time you spend on these big spenders is time well spent.
Continue mailing your best clients and give them reasons to remember you.
Do this when retired and they'll tell their friends about you?
Even in retirement they'll come back and do even more business with you.

**Wholesale contacts in retirement may be more important.**
Others spend time selling and you don't actually sell direct to the client.
Your gallery or dealer does that, and they have the names and addresses.
In this case you are like a wholesale business that markets to retail outlets.
Galleries are clients so treat them as if they buy works directly from you.
Contact them regularly, just as artists who sells direct to the public do.
All the best manufacturers and wholesalers regularly contact retail outlets.
They're very aware of their importance to their profitability.
You should be similarly aware about your gallery, and probably you have.

**When a client is a business a slightly different approach is needed.**
You need to provide business reasons for a purchase.
You commit to saving money, increasing profit, or enhancing your prestige.
Then organize things so that is what is done - be business-like and efficient!
But pay careful attention to people you do not know.
They are prospects but will often take up too much of your time.

**4. It is really great when someone is referred by a previous buyer.**

**When visiting your studio, or gallery, they've been 'sold' on your work.**
But the worst part is waiting for this to happen.
That's why you collect the names and addresses of each of your clients.
Also collect names and addresses of anyone interested in your work.
Write to the buyer or interested person, thank them to show appreciation.
Let them know from time to time of special exclusive opportunities for them.
These won't be available to the general public.

**Never underestimate the power of a good testimonial!**
They establish your credibility and win over potential clients.
Your prospects are impressed by what people like themselves have to say.
This is stronger than anything else on your CV.

**You should use testimonials whenever possible.**
Post reviews and comments from satisfied clients on your website.
It will increase your credibility in the eyes of visitors and encourage sales too.
Effective testimonials can convince your art really **DOES** what you promise.

**Gather quality testimonials and benefit from them immediately:**
Every testimonial should also have a first name, last name, and location.
They help prove the recommendations are coming from real people.
If you already have some positive feedback from clients:
Ask permission to include their comments wherever you plan to do so.
Choose testimonials that tell prospects exactly what they can expect to gain.
To encourage new testimonials:
Add a link to your website so clients to give you their vote of confidence.
For example, "Click here to tell us what you think!"
Contact clients after they've purchased and ask how they're enjoying it.

**When clients send you glowing praise in a letter or email:**
Contact them and seek permission to add it to a website or other promotion.
I do this, even though I may not know exactly where I will use the testimonial.
There's always somewhere that's appropriate.
What if you don't have any testimonials yet?
Offer a work or service free to a group of clients in exchange for thoughts.
Once you have testimonials, include them where they're best suited.

**On your website put your best testimonials on your homepage.**
Insert some testimonials in the middle of your sales copy.

**A page on your site with only testimonials is less effective.**
People skip a page of many testimonials so put them on each website page. More effective as they are relevant to what is on that page - it's that simple!
**Do you collect testimonials?**
Get into the habit for it can be a bit like collecting autographs!

## 4. Your focus is your future.

Reviewed by Mark Jackson – (Springfield, Australia)
1. Focus is the main characteristic of business these days.
2. When retired do less so you have more spare time.
3. Use time management tools.
4. Your focus is your future!
5. But having a focus does not guarantee a successful retirement.
6. Do you have an action plan to take you to retirement?


### 1. Focus is the main characteristic of business these days.

**Trying to be all things to all people is a sure recipe for disaster.**
Walk around a shopping centre and see if this isn't so.

**Many artists expand by adding new prints, or work in another medium.**
**BUT** the better alternative is to specialize even more.
No longer paint domestic animals like cats and dogs, but cat portraits only!
Once you are known for a specialty you'll sell more and for higher prices too.
To be successful you must focus on something.
The same applies if you want to retire successfully!

**Whatever you specialize in have in stock more than anyone else.**
Let's say you specialize in local art.
So more local works available, and be shown to prospects than anyone else.
Not just a few more either, but lots more.
If your main opposition has thirty works to show, aim for several hundred.
You don't need all framed if you work in a small number of standard sizes.
Only with a narrow focus can you stock in depth!
Be an institution, immune from competitors ad set up your retirement income!

**If you specialize in anything then you are in a position to buy cheaper.**
When you retire that will be critical.
If you want 200 frames the same moulding in only three different sizes.
There should be considerable savings from the framer.
They do not have to be constructed at the same time.

**More people will buy from you than your competitors.**
A part of selling cheap is to have a low cost structure.
The cost of selling, expenses and advertising should be closely monitored.
Of course you don't have to sell cheap just make more profit instead!

**You'll own the local art market if you dominate the category.**
Not just more works, but more outlets, too.
Dominate then you'll always be top of the mind with the potential customer.
It's better to have 50% of one market than 10% of five markets!
So narrowing your focus will lead to greater market share and profits.
Be the local artist and dominate the category.
What are you going to dominate at?

**In retirement you'll need to do this to maintain an income stream.**

## 2. When retired do less so you have more spare time.

### In retirement you become more conscious of time.
Unlike an adolescent wasting time you'll know just how precious time is.
So making best use of your time is something you want to do.

### The conventional business wisdom is get as big as possible.
But for a retired artist it is different?
Take a look at your client list.
What would happen if you fired at least half your clients?
Get rid of late payers, give you a hard time or want works for low prices.
They are never the source of positive referrals.
Would your art career improve?
That's what you should focus on in retirement.
Then you'll earn more and spend less time doing it!

### Invest time and energy in activity that give the highest possible return.
Otherwise there is an opportunity cost.
Aim for the top galleries, top prices and top clients.
You'll only need to produce relatively few works.
This strategy is right for your career and essential for retirement.
Do less and earn more.

### In retirement time management is an essential retirement skill.
For example running your own gallery is **NOT** retirement.
It's a change of occupation.

### Time management tools are essential for any professional artist.
They are even more important in retirement!
List all that you are committed to, intend to do, or just would really like to do.
For a typical month in a column on the left hand side of paper or screen.
Include activities like sleep, meals, hobbies, health care, sport, classes, study, reading, relaxation, meetings, don't forget painting, grocery shopping, and so on.
Try to think of everything.
Next to each activity write the time it takes to do each in a typical day.
Round these times off to the closest quarter of an hour.

### Note the number of days per month you do each of these activities.
Some will be every day, but others will be as little as only once a month.
Calculate for each activity the daily time X the number of days per month.
Put this result in another column next to the previous one.
Calculate the total amount of time you need, to do everything on your list.

**Add the numbers in the last column.**
Compare this with the average number of hours available in a month.
A month is 4 weeks, 22 workdays, 8 weekend days with a total of 30 days.
That means there are 728 hours available each month.

**What is the difference between the total required and hours available?**
Do you have credit or deficit time available?
If a time deficit, then changes will have to be made to how you use your time.
You really have no choice.
Make changes at a moderate pace, but do make them.
It's like the tortoise and the hare, slow and steady wins the race.
Things often start simply and get more complex as time goes by.
Use an ideas book, diary, yearly planner and procedures manual.

**Do you have a procedures manual - most artists do NOT.**
Probably most businesses don't either, although large business is likely to.
**BUT** all franchises have a procedures manual, but often different names.
That's also why franchises are a very effective business model.
Everyone knows what they are supposed to do to make the business work.
In retirement it is essential if your business is to carry on when you can't.

**So how should you go about creating one?**
A first step is to develop a computer file with your whole business approach.
Include action steps or procedures that are taken to do anything important.
Important things are those that just must be done right or a poor job results.
It could be things that are done a certain way for that's how you do them.
They could also be things that are only done occasionally.
Write what has to be done means you don't forget how to do them next time.

**That's a lot of work, so it needs breaking down to manageable chunks.**
Initially just create an outline of the main elements of your art business.
You might consider studio operations, marketing, finance, and so on.
Develop a list of procedures (actions) to go with the heading you decide on.
At this stage you just list those procedures.
If you meet a problem, document procedures (steps) to be taken to solve it.
Put that onto your computer file or loose-leaf procedures manual.
If the problem reappears at a later date, refer to the procedure and follow it.
If changes are needed make them and amend or add the new procedure.
Then over time each important procedure gets developed to be even better.

**Document just one procedure a week.**
That adds up to 50 or so in a year!
If they're the most urgent a large chunk of frustrating situations is now gone.

**If you employ anyone (agent) they can contribute in a similar manner.**
Deal with three or four procedures a month (even if there was no problem).
Eventually everything you do each day will be in your Procedures Manual.
What you now have are systems for running your art business.

**Anybody can use it!**
It will also save considerable wastage of your time.
If people want to know how something is done, refer them to the manual.

## 4. Your focus is your future!

### Take specific steps to make your retirement happen!
So whatever you do now you work towards retiring!
Day to day things should be secondary to those longer term objectives.
Otherwise your hopes and aspirations are being left to chance.
Deciding about where you want to head is not just wishful thinking.
Look at what you are doing to-day.
What single service, product, or idea is your best hope for the future?
Ideally it's also the basis for your retirement.

### It's that simple AND it's also hard.
The hard part is making the right selection from the different things you do.
It's hard for you really won't know you've been right until time has elapsed.
By then it's probably too late to return to one of the other options.
Never-the-less this is what you must do.
As time goes by there'll be an upward spiral to support your original decision.
Your focus lets you to develop in ways not previously possible or foreseen.

### But a focus loses power if the environment it operates in changes.
An easy way to illustrate this is to think about the life of some famous artists.
Pierre Renoir was someone whose focus was constant for many years.
Towards the end of his life, failing eyesight meant he re-evaluated his focus.
A different kind of painting emerged.
Many other artists' careers demonstrate this process (Picasso) too.
Those who lived short lives didn't need to adjust focus (Raphael, van Gogh).

### It's not easy to think of artists who changed focus needlessly.
Their career came unstuck and they are not famous but you know them.
Often this was a result of becoming bored with what they currently did.
They did something different, rather than conscious adoption of new focus.
Have a strategy about the general direction of your art business.
It's certainly better to be clear about the focus of the business than lofty aims.
If you do one thing better than anyone else, gets acclaim and is rewarded.

### Focus is not the same as strategy.
Many businesses have a strategy.
They want to become major players in their field for example.
A person considering a career in art, it might be to become a full-time artist.
Anything that can fit within the strategy will do.
On the other hand a focus is about narrowing the perspective of a business.
The intention isn't to cover all eventualities, but dominate a market segment.
There is strength when you can dominate a segment of the market.

**There's no power when you are just a small player in a big market.**
Then you have no control over your destiny as it's shaped by bigger players.
You are like a small leaf floating in a stream.
It may be a pleasant journey, but you've little control over where you end up.

**Some artists wish to master all media.**
There is a challenge in doing that, which is tantalizing.
That's a product of time on a task multiplied by degree of intelligent effort.
A multi-media artist spends a certain amount of time working intelligently.
They use each of the different media and achieve a level of mastery at them.

**Imagine we can clone this artist.**
Now we have one for each of the different media.
Each clone works intelligently for the same time in a single medium.
What will the clones, with exactly the same levels of intelligence, achieve?
Will it be similar, lesser or greater mastery than the original artist?

**It is very difficult to master a range of disciplines.**
**BUT** to be successful as well is infinitely more difficult.
More energy tends to be applied in the less successful areas.
**This reduces time spent on those areas the artist does best.**
The lack of focus reduces the artistic energy applied to any other disciplines.
It is dissipated instead.

**I've only mentioned artistic difficulties but there's marketing problems.**
Artists who try to cover all artistic bases, really doesn't stand for anything.
The more specific the focus of an artist the easier it is to market that artist.
So do you paint in all mediums to a reasonable level?
What can you say that will make you stand out from others like yourself?
What can you say that will make you stand out from specialists in mediums?
**BUT** they will continue to improve at a greater rate than you'll be able to!
You will inevitably be left behind.

**But let's say you paint in oils, local subjects, primarily buildings.**
They have a historical interest, and are all priced between $500 and $2000.
There is a certain range of sizes too.
The more specific you get, the easier you are to promote.
This is basically the case for specialization which a focus makes possible.

**Focus is about less rather than more, just like the laser beam.**
By its nature a focus doesn't cover everything you might be able to do.
It's a point of attack towards the future of your artistic business (career).
It also leads to a fulfilling retirement!

**A focus can and should change as circumstances change.**
Nothing stays the same long enough for you to stay singularly focused.
The objective of your focus should be to lead you in a coherent direction.

**Establish retirement goals, then focus until you have achieved them.**
Do not let your focus slip.
Maintaining focus is the aspect that sorts the professional from the hobbyist.
You make sacrifices if a particular activity does not lead towards your goal.
You will not be diverted from achieving your goal.
You may break down your goal into smaller sub-goals.
Then progressively work at those as you move towards the major objective.
Armies win many battles before the war is won (retirement reached).

**Focus is the characteristic of winners in any field.**
Don't be sidetracked, but stay on your chosen pathway.
This doesn't mean you can't change your focus from time to time.
A focus is the bridge that takes you from to-day to to-morrow.
Now you paint in oils and in the future acrylic is the way for you.
Focus lets you bridge the gap and make change possible, even profitable.

**At any time an artist will have three types of artistic output.**
Yesterday's works.
Today's works, which should be producing the bulk of your profits.
To-morrow's works, which are your future which are also for your retirement.
Focus on what you sell, and what you make money on might all be different.

## 5. But having a focus does not guarantee a successful retirement.

**Well not straight away at least.**
In the short term, narrowing your focus may even cost you opportunities.
You'll turn away chances because they do not fit in your plans.
What if someone wants a watercolour but you are only painting oils now.
Because oils are your focus you turn down watercolour projects in retirement.

**But what works in the short term doesn't tend to work in the long term.**
A business chasing immediate success, is ultimately headed for failure.
You need courage to make a focusing decision and wait for market reaction.
It won't happen overnight, but it will happen - you just have to be patient.
Put another way, persistence is the key to success.
Make the correct decision and then keep moving forward with it.
At first progress is slight, but momentum grows to set up a perfect retirement!

**Finding a focus is easy.**
I have likened a focus to activity, as a laser to light.
Concentrated light is extremely powerful and does things diffused light can't.
It's the same for another power source, your energy.
Focus your energy and you'll achieve what others consider impossible.
Just think about the idea and then decide.
Typical for an artist is to be a good oil painter (pastel artist, whatever).
However the more specific your focus the more you'll become like the laser.
What do you paint, how much will they sell for, how long will this take?

**Then achieve this laser-like artistic goal in a series of small steps.**
Large steps are daunting and you'll probably not get there.
List all the things you do as an artist or are even just part of your interests.
Find those, or their combination, that set you apart from others!

**The laser has power!**
When you have a focus, like the laser, you create a powerful perception.
Perception of value is linked to your focus and it lies in the mind of the client.
Thus a focus is self-reinforcing.
People tend to gravitate to places or businesses, or artists that have a focus.
Cars, jewellery, fashion clothing, telemarketing, gambling red light areas too.

**When you have a focus to your retirement you know what to do.**
You'll know what kind of gallery you are looking for or need to retain.
You'll also know what research to do, what new works to produce, and so on.
Where knowledge is rapidly expanding, a focus is essential to stay on top.

**No one can stay on top of all things.**
**BUT** a focus directs you to those areas most likely to be of benefit to you. In retirement this is essential.

## 6. Do you have an action plan to take you to retirement?

### An action plan is different from a plan.
A plan is just a map.
It shows various elements of what you want to achieve.
An action plan also contains the sequence of steps.
The steps let you put the elements together so you reach your destination.

### Outline a starting point:
Take time to honestly evaluate your current situation.

### Write down your goals:
List of everything you want to accomplish between now and retirement.
Put them into a priority order.
The most important and urgent are placed first.
Then the most important, followed by urgent and everything else after that.

### Develop your plan:
Work out just what you want to do.
This will help you take control of your present situation.
You will also shape up your future in the way you want it to go.

### Decide how you'll deal with setbacks:
Dealing with reverses is never easy, but they are inevitable.
If you are prepared, then they become manageable at least.

### Set milestones:
Break down your overall plan into smaller sections.
Set target dates for when each of the sections will be reached and passed.

### Develop a reward system:
As each smaller goal is reached, reward yourself and continue on your path.

### At regular intervals, review what you have achieved.
Adjust your plan according to your new perspective.
Make the changes that are most important.

### What kind of income would you like when you are retired?
Low maintenance occasional income so you still paint but at a reduced rate.
Reduced maintenance regular income:

### You may need to maintain an income.
**BUT** you no longer wish to pursue actually painting as a way to do this.

**You may not be selling anything which is depressing.**
You may have run out of ideas.
The number of works required to earn a reasonable income is beyond you.

**There might be active Income where you do things.**
Use some of your knowledge and experience.
Some options might include teaching and running workshops.

**But passive income is even better!**
Art hiring means regular payments.
Prints can generate regular income too.
Copyright is money on the table.

**These are proper commercial businesses.**
They will take time and money.
If you are no longer painting you have credibility.
But do you have the money?
Do you really want to spend the time?

## 5. Semi-retired with regular income.

Reviewed by Donald Burrow
1. You want to retire but still need a regular income.
2. What do businesses buy?
3. Selling points for hiring (or renting).
4. Is producing and selling prints feasible?
5. How do you actually sell the prints?
6. Sell drawings

**1. You want to retire but still need a regular income.**

**Your money supply has a BIG bearing on the nature of your retirement.**
If you have an independent income then you need no art sourced money.
You have no need for this career guide either.
What if the money you make still has to come from your reduced art career?
Your money needs might be regular just you don't want to work so hard.

**In this Chapter we'll look at ways to be semi-retired.**
You make money regularly but your career is less active than previously.
To control the flow of your retirement income:
You **MUST** set up the projects described **BEFORE** you retire.
Then they can be continued easily in retirement.

**I know it's been said that money makes money, and that is largely true.**
**BUT** it's also true that you don't need money to make money.
It both statements are true something else is necessary for making money.
**BUT** you must seek opportunities to make money, even in retirement.
If you do not look, you will not find.

## 2. What do businesses buy?

**Corporations buy all manner of artworks.**
Some for boardrooms which are often large and prestigious (a lot of money).
Business also buys a great deal of other smaller less expensive works.
These are for corridors, normal offices, etc.
However, these days most businesses have little money to waste.
They are thus less inclined to buy artworks than a few years ago.

**Are there problems for a business that buys artworks?**
It may be tax-deductible but the claim is not easy to substantiate.
Depreciation reduce the attractiveness of this approach to tax minimization.
Depending where you live, there might be a capital gains tax down the track.

**Have you thought about hiring (renting) art to businesses?**
Our government in Australia has lends work to government departments.
They also lend art to the non-government sector.
I imagine other countries have similar authorities and arrangements.
Any business that is likely to buy paintings is also a candidate for hiring.
The best ones to approach are those with waiting rooms and boardrooms.
Offices and areas where people sit and look at a wall are hiring prospects.
Any business that's conscious of its image is a potential hiring client too.

**So why hire when you can sell?**
With renting or hiring, people pay so much a month, to use the paintings.
I had a number of works hired by a firm of solicitors for over 17 years.
Depending how hiring fees are calculated costs are covered in a year or two.
Everything from then on is pure profit, and you still own the works!

**That's the kind of income you need in retirement – passive income.**
Passive income is money that arrives at regular intervals.
You need to do little more than set it up.
Receiving rent or dividends are well known forms of passive income.
Business people are used to hiring too.
It is a total, legal, tax-deductible expense, if the work is hung at the business.
It's a similar arrangement to hiring cars, or pot plants, or furniture.
The business is paying for the use of these items, but not for ownership.

**They're not stuck with works as they would be if bought outright.**
Offer to take them back (exchange for others) after a time (one, six months).
You've a strong argument, and they don't worry if the selection is criticized.
This is often a concern for people unfamiliar with art.

**Most of my hiring contracts lasted three or four years, often longer.**
Less than two years is rare.
As a result of hiring artworks to businesses, I now have a stock of artworks.
Many are earning me money on a regular basis.

**What rental does the business pay?**
The simple answer is whatever you convince them to pay.
Fees are mainly determined by the size of the work.
They link the retail cost of a work, and the duration of the hiring contract too.
I don't tell the client the retail price.

**I wouldn't allow any of my hire stock to be bought either.**
It's not part of the arrangement so I don't quote a selling price to a business.
This costs $50 a month to hire, others cost the same and some are less.
The longer the contract the better (lower) the rate is.
I recover my share of the cost in two years (i.e. 2/3 of the retail price).
After that the work owes me $0 and any further hiring is 100% profit.
If you are hiring out your own works you could be even more generous.
Generally people pay me about 2% per month.

**Suggested contract duration and related charges:**
LESS THAN 36 MONTHS: 2% a month of current value of work when hired.
MORE THAN 36 MONTHS: 1.5% a month oft value of work at time of hiring.
Just so you get the idea let's take a hypothetical case.
A work is $2000 (you get $1333 or less after deducting gallery commission).
Hiring fee is $40 a month (2% of the value), so in a year you receive $480.
That amount covers the frame, canvas, paint etc. (in other words your costs).
Let's say your costs for this painting were $450.
Once this amount has been passed you are making a profit.
At the end of a second year you make $510 and the end of year three $990.
This is $107 more than your profit from a sale ($1333 - $450).
Continue making another $480 for each additional year that the work is hired.

**If this seems a little confusing so I'll try to explain with more clarity.**
Original cost = $450 a painting for 4 paintings (not mine that's what I paid).
Hire = ($9 per painting per month) $36 per month payment.
But $3.15 per painting per month was tax deductible at a rate of 35%
Real cost = ($9 - $3.15 = $5.85 per painting per month) or $23.40 per month.
There is no extra cost for a rise in value during the hiring period.
Several years down the track the client could be hiring four $900 works.
The actual outlay is $23.40 per month (when the value WAS $450 each).
Later you could reduce long-term clients' fees further as illustrated below.

**BUT if you point out the capital gains values (above).**
You demonstrate the increasing value to the client of continued hiring.
It will cost more to replace these works with equivalent valued works!
There is interest gained on money not spent (varies).
Also the rate of appreciation of the artworks, and the inflation rate.

**Build in incentives to encourage people to become long-term hirers.**
Say take $50 off each year for first five years as a thank you for continuing.
In that example, it would cost $250 to do this but in 5 years your client $2150.
They continues at $430 a year forever, knowing you have given a good deal.
You needn't use these amounts; they just illustrate what you could do.

**Another approach is lock in annual payments rather than monthly fees.**
In the above example you quote an annual fee $480 rather than monthly one.
You could also suggest quarterly or semi-annual payments too.
They sound less than annual payment and could be more beneficial to you.
Payment several times a year rather than small monthly or big annual fee.

**Arrange annual payments from different clients in different months.**
Spread your income out better although that will eventually happen anyway.
A variation is to provide a choice.
This work can be hired for $50 a month or $480 a year.
Business people can do sums so they can work out the option they'll take.
**BUT** quoting monthly payments makes everything seem cheaper.
It is thus psychologically more likely to gain a sale (well hire I mean).
A larger annual fee might frighten a client (or their accountant).

**With enough works hired out, you have a regular income stream.**
This irons out the ebb and flow of normal art-world business transactions.
Any unsold works (everybody has some) can still be part of your hire stock.
**BUT** they can attract the same hire price, as other similarly sized new work.
It makes a great deal of sense to do this if it's at all possible.

### 3. Selling points for hiring (or renting).

**The real cost of hiring is not as great as sometimes thought.**
The outlay is reduced by the business tax rate (which varies).
Tax is claimed at the full hiring amount paid as it's a legitimate expense.
It is not a reduced `buy-out' figure (as in leasing).

**Offering to exchange works is an important selling point.**
Many potential hirers feel they may get tired of the paintings after a while.
So are relieved to know the paintings can be changed.
The longer they keep the works, the less likely they are to change them.
The works become a part of the character of the workplace and its identity.
Frame hired works to match the decor of the business environment.
These works are likely to stay hired for a very long time.
Because they will look as if they belong in that environment.
The main risk with this strategy is that initially you are out of pocket.

**You can also offer to paint special works to be hired by the business.**
Thus you combine commissions with the corporate approach and hiring.
Commissions have a slightly higher fee than similar non-commissioned work.
Are you likely to get back any work that was commissioned and then hired?

**You will have a great deal of unframed work too.**
These are likely to be the cheap lines (posters, prints, calendar pages, etc.).
Different mat-boards can marry the range of works on paper to your frames.
The fee you get will mainly be for the frame as the prints etc. are cheap.
By hiring you earn money from framing.
You also have some cheaper options for public areas, corridors and motels.
So much of your hire stock will be framed which are in standard sizes.
Thus only a limited number of frames are required (see elsewhere).

**To lend artworks on the scale of Artbank requires a huge stock.**
A lot of money is in inventory but you don't have to do things on that scale.
So where does your hire stock come from?
Obviously any of your unsold work could be the basis for your hiring stock.

**Make sure this is not inferior work though.**
You could have been putting away works as your superannuation.
Use these as your hire stock and they earn money rather than just stored.
Cheaper options can be bought or acquired (prints, posters, cards).

### What if the hirer returns the work?
Special frames are in standard sizes so all works fit one or another of them.
You hire any returned work out again and there is no cost with the work at all!
Profit from day one!
You'll wonder why you bothered to sell a work and then paint a replacement.
You wouldn't sell but instead retain them in your hire stock.
This will save you painting and framing replacements.
If they change the works the price might remain the same.
**BUT** it could be altered by starting again with current pieces for similar work.
I'd rather add new paintings to my hire stock, instead of replacing ones sold.

### Whatever income you earn from hiring just keeps on coming.
It's added to as more businesses hire rather than buy.
This income comes if you go on holiday and do not paint, or sick and can't.

### So you see a small amount of work can produce passive income.
The money just keeps coming every month with little extra effort.
This provides the perfect recipe for retirement.

### 4. Is producing and selling prints feasible?

**Do enough people like your images sufficiently?**
If so you have a market you can develop for your retirement.
It's likely these people will like more than one of your works.
They can become future buyers, provided you know who they are.

**Say you make images based on reality or have decorative possibilities.**
You can produce prints of these works whenever you want.
This could be in anticipation of retirement.
You spend quite a deal of money and time, so avoid expensive mistakes.
Your print marketing objective is to sell many artworks, which are identical.
Selling a painting needs one person to want the work and agree to the price.
If many sales are desired price must be reduced to increase selling chances.

**Let's say your paintings usually sell for $1500.**
A print for only $30 will obviously attract more people.
Will a price of $15 make even more sales likely?
You don't have to decide straight away, but have to think along these lines.

**People only have limited space on their walls.**
So the more works they buy, the less likely it is they'll buy more.
This can be a problem if you plan to sell the same people many works.
That's what a print publisher (you) does.
However small works are more easily placed, as are works clients like.

**Plan a suite of prints?**
A suite is a number of linked editions.
They'll usually have similar subject matter.
There could be four, six or eight editions.

**A suite of four images will be a good start.**
All will be done to a common theme, in an identical size and presentation.
For example you may produce a suite of Australian flowers, outback landscapes, old pubs, famous people, or whatever.
**BUT** they must be images that appeal to many people.

**Then plan the number of prints in each edition of your suite.**
How many of each print will there be **BUT** do **NOT** be ambitious.
Do not let the printer talk you into more.
For a first project I suggest is 50 is the very most you would consider.
The psychological cost of selling those additional prints will be high.
It's better to have an edition of 20 sold out, than 495 still to sell.

**Decide on the size of your prints.**
Here I suggest small is beautiful.
Around 30cm x 20cm (12" x 8") is a maximum.
The compact size of each print is designed to make sales easier.
Hanging space for small prints should not be a problem for a potential buyer.
Larger prints also require more expensive framing.
**BUT** a small size contributes to a saleable framed price.

**It may be possible to do a deal with your picture framer for this project.**
They will have little wastage when frame sizes are small and identical.
They should be able to pass some of this saving on to you.
It will not cost as much to produce each print in a small size than if bigger.
Several small prints are produced for the same price as one larger edition.

**Do not take notice of what a printer says about having more printed.**
Do **NOT** think in terms of $ per print (which is what they'll do).
Think in terms of $ per sale.
At this point you've sold none.
It's likely you'll sell the same number whether you get 100 or 1000 printed.

**Print less than you think you can sell.**
Do **NOT** be ambitious.
Make about half of the number you think is reasonable, or less.

**You find a printer who is able to do the job at a reasonable price.**
Decide what you can afford.
If you can have the whole suite printed do so.
However it may be necessary to print only one or two images.
In this case select those you think are likely be the most popular to print first.

### 5. How do you actually sell the prints?

**You have prints probably in one, maybe two editions of a planned suite.**
Here's the really important bit.

## ONLY PUT ONE EDITION ON SALE.

**Any other editions, keep for the future.**
Why do you do this?
Does it mean people have less choice so this make sales less likely?
Well, yes and no.
Yes, it does give people less choice.

**They either have to buy the print offered or none.**
It is possible to lose sales from people would preferred one of the others.
**BUT** it's likely they've bought the one that's for sale.
They didn't know about the others.
So total sales may be down on what they could have been with a choice.
Sales of the print available are most likely up on what they could have been.
So you'll have less of them left, perhaps even none!

**Make the print available for a limited time, publicized very strongly.**
The cut off could be Christmas, next month, Mothers' Day or whenever.
After that don't even leave a single one up.
Then you won't be tempted to sell just one more.
Do that and the credibility of your marketing strategy goes out the window.

**Make sure you capture the name and email address of each buyer.**
This is very important for these people are potential buyers of more prints.
Then next year, they can be contacted early by email.

**Sales of the second print can be made before they go on public sale.**
**BUT** the price will be a little higher.
Although you could make special advance offers if you like.
Consequently, you'll sell some (or even many) prints to past buyers.
In addition to those, you'll also sell other prints from regular marketing.

**Next year make the print available again for a limited time.**
This is carried out in the same way as the first year, publicized very strongly.
Which again means, at a suitable time put the second print edition on sale.
That's after you have satisfied your email clients.
The cut off is the same as before (Christmas, next month, Mothers' Day).
When that date arrives, you remove the unsold prints from sale.

**Perhaps even better they are sold out?**
Again you capture the name and email address of each buyer.

**You sell more this time with two marketing promotions instead of one.**
Another advantage of the compact size now becomes obvious.
Some of the people you've emailed, who wouldn't have otherwise bought.
Now they will create pairs and eventually sets by buying additional prints.
This would be less likely if large prints were sold.

**Repeat this process annually with each print edition.**
You will probably find that some people are collecting the whole suite.

**Some people would like to collect the whole suite but can't.**
They missed out on one of the early prints.
Email them saying you have some early prints, in very limited quantities.
You didn't sell originally are now available, to later buyers, at current prices.

**Using this process you can sell a whole suite of prints.**
You must be patient.
Keep your numbers down.
Keep the sizes small.
Make sure the images have wide appeal.

**If you do your sums you will also find it is well worthwhile.**
More importantly, a print project such as suggested can be expanded.
Even with a second suite offered concurrently to another group of prospects.

**Don't publish too many prints.**
It is important to publish only a minimal number of prints.
However in future years the price may rise a little.
The following figures provide some reasons that underpin that statement.

**It might cost $2500 to publish an edition of 500 = $5 per copy.**
An edition of 1000 might only cost $3 per copy = $3000.
An extra $500 you can print an additional 500 copies saving 40% per copy.
The figures are typical and the principle applies even with different numbers.

**But what if we look at that another way?**
The number of copies available for sale is 500 or 1000.
At the start you have sold none.
Your basic cost is $2500 or $3000.

**When you sell one print it has cost $2500 or $3000.**
When you sell two prints each has cost $1250 or $1500.
After the third sale the cost per print is $625 or $750.
You have to sell the lot (500 or 1000) to recover your costs of publication.

**Of course you mark your prints up for sale (let's say by 100%)**
Now when you sell one print it has cost $1250 or $1500.
When you sell two copies each has cost $625 or $750.
After the third sale the cost per print is $312.50 or $375.
You have to sell half (250 or 500) to recover your costs of publication.
Only then will you start making a profit.

**You will start making a profit sooner on the smaller production run.**
There are fewer copies to be sold before break-even is reached.

**The hardest single part of the whole exercise is making an actual sale.**
People should be pessimistic about the number of sales likely.
Then for production they should cut that in half (at least).

**The very best outcome is to sell the lot!**
The number printed or published relates to the probability of selling the lot.
A small number the more likely that will be the outcome (but not guaranteed).
Producing a single print or copy (at any cost) is the best possibility.
But this may have to be sold at a high price.

**If it is exclusive, as a unique item is, then that may even be possible.**
It will be more possible than selling a very large number (at whatever price).
Only one buyer has to be found (instead of 500 or 1000).
Many paintings sell for $500 or $1000 so it's possible to sell a unique item.

**An edition sold out (even if comprises only one or ten or twenty prints).**
Then selling the next edition is easier (even if it costs more to produce).
If an edition is different (usual) you can sell to the people who bought initially.
If the edition is a re-print, you seek additional buyers (one or ten or twenty).
In either case you have promotional leverage of sold out with the first edition.
Either is easier than selling a second or twenty-first copy of an edition of 500.

**Every unsold print costs you real money.**
You can't just remainder them (for the cost of production) like a publisher.

**A continuous print publishing creates a steady retirement income!**
But selling prints can also mean selling frames!
It is common to sell prints unframed.

**But with low edition numbers framed sales are also feasible.**
If a standard size and style is used framing can contribute to sales and profit.

## 6. Sell drawings

**Most artists have been 'brought up' on drawing as a basic artistic skill.**
Many artists develop a love of drawing as a consequence.
They continue to draw long after their initial learning period.
It's no surprise if we realize there are a huge number of drawings created.
Some done rapidly as sketches, others are studies for works in other media.
Yet others are very carefully rendered works.
A surprise is how hard it is to sell drawings especially for reasonable money.

**We all have stuff in the too hard basket.**
They're good ideas we'll get around to one day.
Maybe they're ideas that seemed good but never quite worked, and so on.
For many artists their too-hard basket contains drawings.
Well retirement is just the time to look at the too hard basket again.

**The huge number of drawings means supply always exceed demand.**
Thus prices are depressed.
Drawing is seen as preparatory for a major work and thus is lesser.
Because it is often student work, many drawings are of student standard.
So all drawings are seen as inferior.

**But these statements do not apply to all artists.**
However, there are enough potential buyers who think like this.
So artists who wish to sell drawings feel the effect.
If you are one of this group what can you do?
But first of all you'll need to accept the sad facts.
You can't get the same return for a drawing as for an equivalent painting.
This has nothing to do with quality of work but buyer perception of value.
Drawings are seen as low value, paintings higher status and higher value.
This attitude is something that has developed over many years.
It's now part of the sociological fabric surrounding art and its marketing.

**There are people who are 'drawers' and not interested in painting.**
If you are in this category then you may have to consider these possibilities.
For many a black and white monochromatic scheme characterizes drawing.
Apply colour to a drawing; say a wash, and the chances of a sale increase.
Colour washes are easy to do, even by 'non-painters'.
More importantly, they do not obscure the essential drawing.

**Drawing in colour is a step further down the track.**
Do your actual drawing in coloured pencil, pastel or ink.
Artists, who like drawing find they let them to produce major works.

**They sell for reasonable or even high prices.**
For artists in this category painting is not essential at all.

**But say you like black and white drawing, as in charcoal or pencil?**
Well you can vary this just a little by keeping your work monochromatic.
Sepia works would sell a little better than black and white for example.
They also retain all of the basic drawing character.

**What about making your drawings into prints?**
This doesn't mean you have to learn etching or lithography, but you could.
Make reproduction prints easily and cheaply from drawings on a photocopier.
You have to sell many images rather than one but each can be sold cheaply.
The total has potential to be much greater than a single drawing sale.

**Another idea is to keep your drawings small.**
This means less time spent to produce the work and framing is inexpensive.
Prices can be kept down.
It's the expensive drawings that are usually the hardest to sell.

**Do you paint as well as draw?**
If that's the case, then all of the above suggestions can work for you.
**BUT** there are some other approaches too.

**If most of your drawings are studies for major paintings.**
Then they're marketable with the paintings themselves.
Yes, sell the studies with the major work.
A package, someone buys the work and for an additional sum, the study.
Also exhibit the studies at the same time as the major work.
But they are sold for less money.
The presence of the major works will help sell the studies.

**You can even give drawings away.**
Hey, what's going on here, I can hear you say!
Well the important thing is that you get something for the drawings.
It does not necessarily have to be cash.
You could give a study (unframed?) away with a painting bought.
What you receive is a higher amount this strategy attracts for your paintings.
Which would you rather sell a painting or a study?

**Give a framed study to a charity.**
You help the organization, get exposure and have expensive work to sell.
You can even barter studies and sketches for goods (framing?).
If you make enough sketches, it's not essential to get high prices for each.

**There is one other way you can market drawings too.**
Just produce drawings and nothing else.

**Make your mark as an artist who draws!**
Your USP (see elsewhere) will definitely include drawing.
You will draw in a variety of sizes, as a painter does.
Your pricing will reflect the different sizes too.
So more complex drawings are in the larger sizes and attract highest prices.
This is hard at first, but stick to it and sell drawings for reasonable money.

**Selling drawings is an excellent strategy for your retirement.**
They don't take long to do and can set up steady income.

## 6. Occasional money in semi-retirement.

Jennifer Marshall – (Warwick, Queensland)
1. In retirement you have other income sources.
2. Sell the copyright to your works.
3. Why do most artists fail to exploit copyright?
4. Who are likely buyers of copyright?


## 1. In retirement you have other income sources.

**You are semi-retired with a career but your activity is reduced.**
Thus your money supply might be sporadic (unpredictable).
That means it has to be supplemented from time to time.

**Maybe you just want to work professionally when you feel like it?**
Whatever the circumstances there are ways to earn money occasionally.
Set up these projects when your career is active.
Then you will be able to continue with a reduced time penalty in retirement.

**Copyright is the right to copy an original creative work.**
Is not limited to art works, it applies to literature, musical scores and so on.
With literature selling copyright is the main way authors make money.
Publishers pay for the right to copy the author's story in a book form.
The author keeps the manuscript, or original work.
It has some value, but not as much as the copyright.

**How does copyright relate to owning a painting?**
Copyright exists in relation to any artwork.
The artist owns the artwork and the copyright.
They may be sold together or separately.
Many artists do not realize this, thinking they automatically sell both together.
Most buyers do not realize this either, although publishers do.

**You automatically own copyright, except as outlined next paragraphs.**
You may assign copyright to someone else.
When you die the copyright will pass to someone else, often your family.
Copyright is just like any other property you own at the time of death.

**An exception is if you create a work as part of your employment.**
Then the employer is the owner of copyright to that work.
Perhaps you are paid as photographer for the local newspaper.
Copyright on photographs taken in your duties, is owned by the newspaper.
If you work freelance then you own the copyright.

**There is a second exception to ownership of copyright by the creator.**
A photograph, portrait or engraving created in return for payment (or benefit).
In this case, the client is usually the first owner of copyright.
This is a commission arrangement although this does not apply for paintings.

**A third exception is work created for or first published by government.**
Then government usually is the first owner of copyright, even if it's a painting.
Well you'd expect something like that from government wouldn't you?

**Selling the artwork does not automatically sell the copyright.**
An artist owns copyright unless it is specifically transferred to someone else.
Copyright ownership gives an owner legal right to copy an original artwork.
It's the right to copy that's owned not necessarily the work itself.
A common situation for copyright to be sold by an artist is to a publisher.
The publisher produces prints of the work, say in a book, magazine or cards.
Someone bought a painting but they can't have cards produced.
Perhaps you aren't worried about this, but you do own the copyright.
You can produce cards of your paintings, owned by someone else.

**When selling copyright, it can be transferred in a limited way.**
Sell copyright for a particular image for certain types of reproduction process.
This is **NOT** for any other kind.
This could be a publisher has copyright to produce placemats of a painting.
If they want to produce cards then they must negotiate again.
You can even sell that form of copyright to someone else.

**Limitations can also apply in other ways too.**
A common limitation is the number to be produced.
The publisher can produce (say) 1000 prints.
If they want to make more they must renegotiate.
Geographical limits can also apply.
The prints can only be sold in Australia, London, or where you care to name.
World rights are still to be negotiated.

**Copyright is owned by you.**
Unless there's a written signed document assigning copyright or part thereof.
Which says someone else owns copyright or some portion thereof.
A circle containing the letter 'c' with the name of the copyright owner,
Tells people a work is copyrighted **BUT** it is protected without the symbol.
Permission, short of complete copyright is usually called license.
Permission is needed to reproduce just part of one of your works.
If the part is important in relation to the whole work.
It is not permissible to reproduce a work just making changes (alter colour).

## Can you compare a work and copy and important parts identified?
Then your permission to copy is necessary.
This is scanning an image on a computer and altering it to make a new work.
If by someone other than you.
Copyright owner's permission is needed to copy an image and also to alter it.
Even if no intention to publish the copy, people still need permission to copy.
It's about copying rather than what's done with the copy.
It is possible for art galleries or museums to copy a work for archival records.

## How long does copyright last?
Copyright expires on your works 50 years after your death.
This applies no matter who owns copyright and expired it can't be revived.
There may be more than one copyright to some works.
A photograph of a painting has copyright to the painting and photograph.
These situations can be changed by agreement between the parties.

## A commissioning client, who is not the owner of copyright,
Is entitled to use the work for the purposes for which it was commissioned.
They will need the copyright owner's permission for any other purpose.
A publisher who commissioned you to paint a series for reproduction.
Say on place mats, can't just publish prints as well, without your permission.
Giving the added permission may mean new terms are negotiated.
It follows that the owner of a work may not be the owner of copyright.
The work owner can sell, exhibit or donate the work, not the copyright owner.
When selling copyright you can ask for attribution.
You should be recognised as the creator of the original work.
Even if you don't ask for this, there's an obligation on the copyright owner.
You can ask that any copy be faithful reproductions.

## Publishers of digitized material often publish works at low resolution.
This allows viewing on a screen but doesn't produce a good printed copy.
You could insist on this as a way of discouraging unauthorized reproductions.
But you may not want a work published any way other than full resolution.
It's up to you, but the copyright holder must know what the situation is.
You could insist information about copyright is published in a digitized image.

## It's a good idea for permission to be in writing.
The documentation shows what exactly is covered by the agreement.
Who is giving permission (you) and who receives?
You should state you are the owner of copyright.
You haven't granted rights to the work inconsistent with the agreement.
You could offer compensation if this information is later found to be incorrect.
It costs you nothing, but provides some protection for the copyright buyer.

## An assignment of rights:
You could give new ownership of copyright, or an exclusive license.
This might entitle the new owner to sue for infringement by someone else.
This must be in writing to be legally valid.

## Describe the work(s) to which copyright is being assigned.
You could supply a copy of the work (photograph) as part of this description.
Set out clearly what you are giving permission for the copyright buyer to do.
You can assign or license just some of the copyright rights.
It's also possible for you to retain some specified rights and sell all else.
You may give exclusive rights or a non-exclusive license.
Set out what is the case.

## How long does the permission to copy last?
It may be for the full period of copyright or something less (a sunset clause).

## What territory is covered?
It may be local, in Australia or wherever you decide and they agree on.

## What do you get?
Set out your payment and/or other benefit that you get from the arrangement.
It goes without saying it's a good idea to receive some benefit from the sale.
Money is the best benefit, but there are other possibilities.
You should also say when you are to receive this.
On signing the document is best.
You can set out requirements for attribution, and in regard to any alterations.
You could also state what they should do to prevent unauthorized copying.
This may be difficult to prevent when images are digitized.

## Finally sign and date the agreement.
Both you and the other party need to do this. vii. International treaties.
Australia is a party to a number of international copyright treaties.
You'll be protected in those countries, which are parties to the agreements.
For this reason copyright in New Zealand, is much the same as Australia.
You'll need to check in your country to ascertain if there are differences.

## 2. Why do most artists fail to exploit copyright?

**Selling copyright can be a very attractive proposition.**
An artist may keep the painting, now worth more, and receive income too.
Successful reproduction print artists can be very well rewarded.
You'd be surprised at how well some print artists live, but it is competitive.

**What are the advantages in retirement?**
Many advantages flow from selling copyright, quite apart from the money.
Not the least is considerable promotion by wide availability of your images.
You can benefit by sales of original works too, not just those in prints.
Copyright is worth real money, but is seldom exploited by most artists.
Usually artists only sell copyright to a publisher.
It's no easy task to make such a sale.

**There's a huge number of artworks even if we don't know how many.**
How many of them have provided money to the artist for the copyright?
Not too many in comparison to the number painted, is it?
Not even compared to the number sold!
Most artists receive no money at all for this sellable part of their art activity.
That's because they believe there's only one way to get money for copyright.
That's by selling to a publisher.
**BUT** there is another way.
It's something you probably have never heard about before, anywhere.

**Remember selling the artwork does NOT automatically sell copyright.**
You own the copyright unless it is specifically transferred to someone else.
Can you earn money from copyright without publishing at all?
Each time you sell artworks have the copyright for sale, for a small premium.
Perhaps 10% is a reasonable premium for copyright, but it's up to you.
That's what authors get when they sell copyright.

**A person buys a work for $1000 and for an extra $100 gets copyright.**
It could be $1100 work has $100 for copyright just approach how you wish.
You could promote ownership of copyright in this way as an add-on bonus.
Owners like to know they can reproduce a work, even if they never do.

**Notice you will receive 10% extra income for NO extra work.**
Well, not quite, for not all people will want the copyright, but many will.
Whatever the number, it's still extra money just for asking.
It's money you would not otherwise have obtained.
But a client is paying extra and receiving something valuable to them.

**Are there are other advantages too?**
Let's say someone wants to buy your work, but at a discount.
In this day and age it's happening more and more often.
Well then, you say 'OK I'll sell it to you, but without the copyright.'
You now have an extra bargaining chip.
It's something extra you can take off.
A sale at the full price for your painting (but with copyright) is now more likely.

**You might worry about what people now owning the copyright will do.**
There's not much bad they can do, unless you have sold a terrible painting.
That sort of painting should be destroyed rather than sold anyway.

**Most buyers would do absolutely nothing.**
However ownership of copyright adds value to the painting.
That's because the owner may sell it on at a later date.

**What if a buyer did do something?**
Perhaps they had a set of cards printed!
This only promotes you and has not cost you anything.
It can only do you some good.

**If you believe certain kinds of promotion are good and others are not.**
Then you may not be interested in selling copyright at all.
**BUT** you will forgo income if you take this pathway.
Now at least you have a choice.

**You can sell copyright in a limited way too.**
Thus you can prevent what you consider to be undesirable promotions.
**BUT** still obtain money from your asset.
For example the copyright holder may not use your image on a poster.
Limitations may be a number of copies (one, five, one hundred, whatever).
There may be geographic limits to sales of copies (no local, in your state).
There may be any other limitation that you and the potential owner agree on.

**Limitations reduce attractiveness for the buyer.**
The copyright holder must be able to reproduce your work in some way.
You construct a deal, but there must be something attractive to the buyer.
Otherwise they haven't really obtained copyright.

**Don't forget your own copying needs?**
What if there's a particular work you would like to make a print of yourself?
Just don't let the copyright go or reserve this aspect of copyright for yourself.

## What about value adding too?
Selling copyright is a powerful added value factor that will bring extra sales. As well as extra income from each sale and it really costs nothing to try. Selling copyright to buyers was suggested by me in 'Art Professional' 016. It's an idea that, to my knowledge, has never previously been suggested.

### 3. Who are likely buyers of copyright?

**It's someone who wants to make copies.**
But it's also the person who wants to own the original work!

**Are there other copyright buyers?**
There's another large group of people who are potential buyers of copyright.
What about selling copyright to people who have already bought your work!

**Yes, sell to people who already own your paintings.**
Contact all who bought your work in the past and offer them the copyright.
This could be either outright or a limited version, as you choose.
Sell the copyright for; say 10% of the work's value.

**This isn't easy, as you won't know all past buyers or where they are.**
In addition not everyone will want to buy copyright, for they have the painting.
Say you discover 30% of your past buyers and 25% of these are interested.
Your work sold at an average of $500, and you sold 900 works to 850 clients.

**What could this mean to you?**
It means you've found 255 people who've bought $13,500 worth of paintings.
Of these 64 buy copyright on $3375 worth of paintings.
Copyright sales at say 10% of value will thus bring in $337.50.
The figures are mythical, but I think you'll get the idea.
$337.50 for $120 or so in stamps and a little more for envelopes and paper.
Do it by email and the cost is even less.

**Those most likely to be interested are also likely to be known.**
Buyers of more expensive works and multiple buyers are easier to track.
Than once only buyers of less expensive works.
Taking these factors into account the figures are likely to be much better.
Real figures are likely to be at the upper end of your price scale.

**What about the steak knives?**
Not only can capitalize on sales already made, but do it at to-day's values!
Because you are selling copyright **NOW**, sell it at 10% of the current value.
For example a work sold in 1980 for $500 is now worth $2000.
Apply this thinking to the previously mentioned figures.
The possibility of selling copyright to past buyers looks more attractive.

**You capitalize on rising prices for your work from early buyers.**
They bought cheaply but for copyright they pay on their works value to-day.
Early works could be worth more for the copyright than the original sale price.

**As before most copyright buyers will do absolutely nothing with it.**
But they're getting added value from their original purchase.
Copyright buyers that do something promote you at no cost to yourself.

**Is there a painting you really would like to make a print of yourself?**
Just don't sell the copyright, or you reserve that aspect to yourself.
Use the ideas from the previous Chapter to produce and sell your own prints.

**The more you think along these lines, the more attractive the idea is.**
Even better, it costs you only a little extra to do.
It's still a little difficult if you can't sell paintings in the first place though.

# 7. A hobby artist.

Reviewed by Raisha Rezac – (Beresford, United Kingdom)
1. Many artists run their own gallery in retirement.
2. Can you make money from teaching?
3. What about running a workshop or demonstration?
4. How could you organize a workshop?


## 1. Many artists run their own gallery in retirement.

### It's your choice for that's what being retired is all about!
Everyone has to balance business, family, leisure and anything important.
None of this is simple or easy, but it should be done.

### Distinguishing a hobby artist from a professional is not new.
A hobby artist's only task is to paint paintings (or what their art might be).
You paint when you like, what you like and selling the result is optional.
A hobby view of art does not need to consider running a business.
Whereas a professional artist must.

### People make better use of their time than others by better planning.
**BUT** you are retired so be a hobby artist and produce some paintings.
You could even produce no paintings at all.
It all depends on your income and I'll assume you need some income.

### You'd like to get it from artistic sources.
For that is something where you have some knowledge and experience.
But you really don't want to get into the selling paintings rat-race again.

### Many artists run their own gallery.
Everything is for sale as in any other commercial gallery.
People visiting must be educated about how the gallery itself functions.
Literature is available so people can refer to it, often when they leave.

### Here's a different approach as a way of organizing a gallery.
I call this the Market oriented gallery as opposed to a Viewer oriented gallery.

### What is the viewer-oriented gallery like?
A Viewer oriented gallery is emphasizes VIEWING the artworks.
Special care is given to lighting, how the works are hung, and so on.
National, State and regional Galleries are all set up this way.
The emphasis is on the works and their presentation.
In fact most galleries are set up and operate using this philosophy.

**But the Market oriented gallery is set up to SELL artworks.**
Anything done is so it will help sell the works, whether on display or not.

**It's like the difference between a library and a book-shop!**
One difference could be the labels that are attached to, or near, each work.
In a viewer-oriented gallery they are usually very informative.
Title, media, measurements, date, artist's name is almost always provided.
Often there's a price and biographical or critical information as well.

**But the Market oriented gallery may have NO label, or merely a title.**
A viewer has to seek out information provided in the Viewer oriented gallery.
So the viewer has to become engaged in a conversation with a sales person!
Lack of information helps a sales person identify interested potential buyers.
Too much information and potential buyers are anonymous unless they buy.
The opportunity to turn potential buyers into actual buyers is lost.

**Will some things be the same?**
Say you want to make your gallery a more efficient way of selling artworks?
Do you still do many things that are carry-over from viewer-oriented gallery?
Of course you do, but you should think things through.
For example it's quite likely, when you are open, anybody can come in.
What's wrong with that you might say?
It is inefficient use of your time to be just waiting in case someone comes in.

**In addition, many people who visit galleries are lookers.**
This is not too surprising, for that's how we enjoy art isn't it?
But if they have no intention of buying, in the motortrade they're 'tyre-kickers'.
A car salesman doesn't waste time on tyre-kickers as they don't buy.

**A Viewer gallery is set up to attract lookers or artistic tyre-kickers.**
In addition, wouldn't it be better if only buyers, or potential buyers, came in?
As it stands you have to sort the people out, after they arrive.
Instead you could be operating by appointment.
Accountants, solicitors, hairdressers, and other professionals' value time.
You must make an appointment to use their services.
This is not usual in galleries, but some do, so why not at your gallery?

**You could have a section of your gallery open to the general public.**
Then only at certain times according to your marketing plans.
In other words have people calling when you want them.

**With a Market oriented gallery the focus is on Exhibitions.**
That's because they are the best chance for bulk sales for your other artists.

## Would the gallery layout be different?
A welcome area, people have cups of tea, coffee, a drink and food to eat.
A place for relaxation prior to an interview with yourself or a sales person.

## Consulting areas where you or your consultants can meet with clients.
Here you'll ascertain their needs which could be specialized for each client.
Such as framing, hiring, buying or other services consultations.
There could be folders showing carefully selected samples.
They might be work by your artists, available for hire or examples of framing.

## A VIP area, which is a special area.
This is set aside for free use by your VIP clients.

## An exhibition gallery.
Is open to the public from the opening until the closing of an exhibition.
From hanging until the opening, viewing is **ONLY** available by appointment.

## A preview area, where works for upcoming exhibitions are on display.
Just like in picture-theatres in foyer near the Exhibition Gallery.

## Small Mini-View galleries with work by other artists, or for hire.
Access to these is by appointment only, or a result of consultation with staff.
A Resale gallery is available for public viewing at any convenient time.

## Are you getting the idea?
Your studio could be set up this way too, if you sell from there.

## 2. Can you make money from teaching?

**Maybe your art knowledge can earn regular income?**
The right qualification you can teach in schools, colleges and universities.
What if none of these are possibilities?
**BUT** you still want to teach **OR** you need extra money?
That means you'll have to start your own art classes.

**The start of the year brings is the idea of classes.**
It's certainly a way to supplement income and be rewarding in its own right.
The best teachers enjoy it and obtain satisfaction helping students.

**BUT there are advantages in doing it yourself?**
You can conduct them at times that suit you.
Teach what you know best, rather than a curriculum determined others.
But it's a business you'll be running, not a hobby.
That means you must receive sufficient money to make it worthwhile.

Here is **a link to a book that can provide a course to teach from:**
http://www.amazon.com/dp/1731347324
An alternative is to **use this link to an ebook:**
http://www.amazon.com/dp/B07KK3Y9F5

**Too many artists are paid poorly for teaching, they don't ask enough.**
Price for the service is what others charge or wouldn't pay more themselves.
They spend hours preparing and teaching and are not adequately rewarded.

**People in business pay $hundreds or $thousands, for one day courses.**
Business people recognise the value of what they learn, better than artists.
Often these courses are attended by hundreds of people!
Artists don't usually have the money to spend that business people might.

**Just to make sure you get the idea, let's do some sums.**
A one-day course attracting 250 people at $250 a head will gross $52,500!
With that kind of money it's possible to advertise the course well.
You could even provide meals!
Do a top notch job and you can do it all again next week, somewhere else.
You don't need to run too many courses like this to make serious money.

**By contrast, an artist might charge $5, for a three-hour session.**
This course is for 35 weeks of the year and earns $175 per student per year.
Typically the artist has 10 students as they can't deal with more than this.
However after 10 weeks there are only five students left.

**In this scenario, the artist receives around $1125.**
You'd really have to love teaching or be desperate for money, wouldn't you?
Somewhere between the extremes suggested above, there is a better way.
It may not be possible to obtain business money, but use their thinking.
Then make better money than you otherwise might.

**Ask for your money up front.**
In other words people have to pay for the whole course before they start.
That's what happens at schools, and universities, and in business.

**People who pay weekly only have a weekly commitment.**
That has to be renewed each week.
If people pay for the whole course at the start, you reduce the drop off rate.
This is because people have made a commitment to go the distance.
People pay in advance so you don't have to collect money each week.
You can focus on your teaching, rather than money collecting.
That means now you can plan ahead and actually do some serious teaching.

**If people pay in advance means you receive all money you anticipate.**
You can spend a bit to make your course better if you want.
There'll probably still be some drop off to contend with.
There's always external circumstances over which you've no control.
If you are incompetent, people will not keep coming, even if they've paid.
Although eventually no-one will enroll in your future courses.
Either way you don't lose money this year.

**Paying in advance means people have to pay more money all at once.**
It may be more difficult to find $500 than $5, particularly early in the year.
Cope with this situation by becoming more professional.
Provide credit card facilities.
People pay up front with their credit card at what they're comfortable with.

**You can offer discounts too.**
For example, say you want $600 from each student.
Price your course fee at $900 and offer 1/3 off if paid before the course start.
Many people will find the money to save $300.
Perhaps you could even offer a weekly fee, but make it quite expensive.
Then it's not very attractive.
Let's say $35 a session.
If there's 35 sessions in a year, someone paying weekly will pay $1225.

**Paying by credit card with early payment discount is common sense.**
$600 represents less than half the price of paying weekly.

**Set your courses up like this.**
You'll be surprised at how few weekly paying students you'll have.

**Are you paid what you are worth?**
It's you who decides the price of your expertise, time and the course itself.
If you don't think that's worth much, fine, then don't charge much.
Fortunately there are people who prefer paying higher prices for a course.
They think it's a better standard of tuition so you must deliver on expectation.

**It's time for some more sums, just to make sure you get the picture.**
Your new, well-promoted, course still runs for 35 weeks.
Everyone pays up front so it doesn't matter if there's a drop off or not.
You'll receive $6,000 from ten students who receive the 1/3 discount.

**$6,000 is from 10 students whether the course is 3 hours a week or 2.**
You'll also receive it whether the course runs for 35 weeks, or 30, or even 40.
These become items you can adjust to suit your course plans.
If you think two hours is the ideal time, then that's what you do.
If four ten-week terms work out most desirable, then do that.
It's your choice to charge for the course rather than an hourly or session rate.
Obviously if you can have more students you can earn more money.

**Would you like the steak knives too?**
Larger classes, or additional classes, can be offered.
Attract enough people to run eight classes you earn $48,000 a year teaching.
That's quite a good income for only 16 hours a week for 35 weeks a year.
In addition, you'll get this income all at once, at the start of the year.
So you can do something with the money to produce even more income!

**I'm not saying you should charge the amounts I've suggested.**
They are examples of what is possible but you could ask for more or less.
But if you charge much the same as everyone else.
Most people will tend to think you are about as good as everyone else too.

**Charge more, people assume you must be better than everyone else.**
Particularly if you charge a great deal more than the competition.
If your students think you are better, it's a major factor helping you be better.
The more you charge the better job you'll have to do.

**I can also say the ideas suggested here do actually work.**
I've tested them myself.
Eventually your teaching program decides if people keep coming back or not.

**Have you ever heard of a course guarantee?**
What about offering a guarantee with your course!
Perhaps 'If you don't find this course worthwhile, get your money back.'
Or 'Money back after six weeks if you haven't improved!'
Structure your guarantee whatever way you like, but offer one.
What other art class offers a guarantee?
What other any kind of class or course offers a guarantee?
As soon as you do this, your course lifts itself above any alternatives.

**Most people enroll in a course hoping it will be great.**
These high expectations are one of the main causes of dropping out.
Most courses can't meet that unrealistic level of expectation, neither can you!

**A guarantee helps with this problem, as it takes people's worry away.**
'If it doesn't work out, well I can get my money back.'
With nothing to lose the student is relaxed about the course from the start.
This will be even better if you link your guarantee to a long time frame.

**'Your money back, if after 6 months you haven't learnt something new.'**
The pressure is off you and them to start at an unrealistic level.
You can build their skills and knowledge gradually, but surely.
What does your guarantee tell students?
A guarantee also tells people you are confident about what you do.
You wouldn't offer a guarantee unless you were, would you?
Well actually you would!
A guarantee puts some pressure on you to perform to students' expectations.

**Even more importantly, a guarantee is a way you'll get more students.**
If someone has a choice between two courses, both seemingly equal.
But one offers a guarantee, it's obvious which they'll choose.
They'll select the course with the guarantee, even if it's more expensive.
That's because they can get their money back if it doesn't deliver.
It also helps to combat non-course alternatives that people might consider.

**Offering a guarantee is a very powerful incentive.**
This is particularly strong when other people don't!

**When can your guarantee apply?**
You have a choice between an input and an output guarantee.
An input guarantee guarantees the input the students will receive.
We guarantee you'll receive tuition from a fully qualified tutor, ten painting trips, no more money to spend (you supply material), or other things.
A problem is other people may provide the same things (no guarantee).

**An output guarantee is about what they'll receive.**
You'll learn ten new ways to paint in oils; you enjoy the course.
A discernable improvement or any other outcome you consider likely.

**How long a period should your guarantee cover?**
As long as possible!
A short guarantee means people judge if a benefit has been received quickly.
Most benefits from any course will take time to appear (they do the lessons).
**So a longer guarantee is more appropriate.**
With a long guarantee (six months) there is a good chance people forget.
They are now involved in the course anyway.

## 3. What about running a workshop or demonstration?

**Lots of artists are involved in demonstrations and workshops.**
It's a way they supplement their retirement income and help fellow artists.
If you live in an area with a large population you can make some money.

**When will this happen?**
What time of the year, day of the week and what time is best too?

**Where would be a good place?**
Can you obtain such a place, in your town, city, suburb, area would be best?
What exactly do you need and are you flexible?

**What should you earn if you do?**
If you organize demonstrations and workshops yourself, you earn more.
Than doing these for some organization, as obviously there's more to do.
You'll need considerably more organizing skills than for doing your own thing.

**What will it cost you?**
How much do you want to make?
How many people do you need there?
What is the most you can handle?
What is the least number you need to still make money?
What will it cost them (there may be costs above your charge)?

**What are you going to do?**
Now you are sure why you are having demonstrations or run workshops.
Make certain you set it up to do, just that.
There's no point running demonstrations as a way of making money.
If the approach you plan to use, means there's none, or not enough money.
If you provide people with value for money, almost any goal can be achieved.

**Why will people want to see this demonstration?**
Have you practiced sufficiently?
How long does it take?
Can the time taken vary?
Will you need to supply notes or other handouts?

**You can organize things yourself and approach the general public.**
Sit down and think for a while.
Write down answers to any questions.

**See how they fit together.**
Make sure you test answers against reasons for doing the demonstration.
You should have planned a suitable demonstration and written it all down.
You might need to shuffle the ideas around.
So they are in a more sensible order than at first.

**Read through it like someone attending your course.**
Particularly the kind of person you want to attract.
Have you covered everything they'd want to know?

**O.K. now you've planned a suitable demonstration or workshop.**
Write it all down.
Read through it from the point of view of someone attending your course.

**Have you covered everything they'd want to know?**
For example will it be practical?
Who supplies the materials?
If it's the student, what do they need to bring?
Double-check everything.
Then write it out in several different ways.

**Why several different ways, you may ask?**
Well each different way will tend to suggest some new ideas for you to use.
You need different methods for potential TAFE or art society attendees.
Many of the students may be the same, but the organizations are different.
They operate in different ways, which you need to take into account.
You'll need to be aware of these differences when setting your course fees.

**Have you planned a marketing campaign?**
The next thing you need to do is plan a marketing campaign.
It will be to sell your proposal to the group concerned.
Who do you need to contact?
When is the best time?
It may be late in the year for next year, or a month or so ahead of the course.

**What sort of courses would they be interested in?**
Is yours a fit or different?
What is your background?
Why should they use you?
What can you do for them?
**The last one is the really important one.**
Once you have all this worked out then approach the different groups.
Naturally you'll need different approaches for each.

**They have your proposal and are interested, what next?**
Follow up, that's what!
Do they need any extra information?
Ask when they will have decided what to do.
Give them a ring at about then, or a little sooner, to see how things are going.

**Let's say they don't go ahead with your beaut workshop.**
Find out what the problem was.
There could be any number of reasons.
Do this politely.

**This information will help you prepare a better proposal next time.**
So re-work your ideas and present them again at an appropriate time.
Maintain contact, to find out about workshop ideas they **ARE** interested in.
**AND** which you also can do.

**The next thing you need to do is plan a marketing campaign.**
This is to get people to come to your demonstration.
Who do you need to contact?
When is the best time?
How will you do it?
What is your background?
Why should artists come to your demonstration?
What can you do for them?

**Can you do it?**
Best of luck, for it is fun and you can make money.

## 4. How could you organize a workshop?

### Who will want to attend?
How are you going to reach the people who should attend?
Have they seen something like your demonstration before?
### What will attract them to your course?
Where will you find the people who would like your demonstration?

### Workshop
Use recognised & experienced artists and teachers.
### Students
Generally hobby and semi-professional artists.
Occasionally professional artists.

### Format
Week-end (2 days)
Lunch & morning/afternoon tea each day.
No enrollment after (close date)
No extra materials to be bought.
Maximum might be 15 whilst the minimum is the break/even number.
Do things regularly e.g. at Easter, Xmas, end of financial year, etc.
Include research component so you learn something each time.

### Incentives:
Free Report for early bird enrollers.
Extra Discount for special groups (you decide).
Leverage schools, magazines, art societies and other groups.
Sell before course (e.g. at this course pay for the next one) at reduced price.
Up-sell future courses (block of 4 for price of 3)
Add-Ons - art materials
Cross-sell Reports, tapes, videos, artist's prints, art supplies, etc.

### Follow Up:
Questionnaire after course.
Mailing list now for future so can sidestep societies, schools, etc.

### Collect all money up front.
Standard price for all courses.
$150 per person for both days.
No extra materials to be bought.

**Discounts**
If paid by early bird date ($100)
Pay for next course at reduced price
Future courses (block of 4 for price of 3)
10% for group of 5 or more book together.
Kickback for people who get others to attend

**Add-Ons**
Free Report for early bird
Gift art materials from your stock
Lunch & morning/afternoon tea

**Extras**
Accommodation
Out of town students stay at same venue.
Teacher stays at venue (arrange a contra deal with accommodation) for you
or someone else.

**What do students receive?**
**Tuition**
Written course notes
List materials needed

**Discounts**
If paid by early bird date ($100)
Pay for next course at reduced price
Future courses (block of 4 for price of 3)
10% for group of 5 or more book together.
Kickback for people who get others to attend.

**Free**
Report for early bird
Artist's story (you or teacher).
Gift art materials from your stock
Lunch & morning/afternoon tea

**Extras**
**Accommodation**
Out of town students stay at same venue.
Teacher stays at venue (if contra deal)

**What does a teacher get (you or someone else)?**
**Artist**
Stress importance of actual teaching ability as well as artistic ability.
Standard artists payment
For all courses.
$500 for artist (flat fee any number of students to 15)
No other fee, no expenses
You pay all expenses
Stay with you if contra deal not organized

**Supplies**
'My Story' which is their own story.
Course notes and materials needed with alternatives
Who would benefit from this course?
commonsense advice
professional tuition
practical help
or whatever.

**What you need to do (even if not the teacher)?**
Develop mailing lists
High schools
Art societies
Art teachers
Artists as attendees

**Write and print literature.**
Headings **MOST** important
Focus on factors that qualify the client (sort them out).
**Pre-sales literature.**
Designed to contact people who would benefit most from this course.
Focus on what's in it for them, which are the benefits.
Be specific ... which means that .. (key benefit).
Value factors. (training, skill, commitment, status, their investment,
testimonials.
Say how you'll meet their needs.
Use photographs and cartoons.

**State offer**
Assume everyone is interested and will come.

**Call for action**
Tell people what to do.

**After-sales literature**
Similar to pre-sales literature
Except, designed to help student explain to others, answer questions, adds to knowledge

.

**Double check everything to make sure this is what you do.**

## WHERE NEXT:

BUT being a professional artist is NOW harder than it ever was. These books are on earning money from a professional art career.

**GALLEY CO-OPERATION Take the plunge.**
http://www.amazon.com/dp/B087637FFW

**SELLING STRATEGIES helps people buy.**
http://www.amazon.com/dp/B0882JH3WN

**MAKE EXHIBITIONS WORK then set up a sell-out!**
http://www.amazon.com/dp/B0882MFPGX

**ART HIRING beats selling!**
http://www.amazon.com/dp/B0884JWR2S

**COURSES AND WORKSHOPS and teaching earns money!**
http://www.amazon.com/dp/B0884B51JB

**AGENTS help productivity.**
http://www.amazon.com/dp/B08847Y9KS

**YOUR WEBSITE gets referrals.**
http://www.amazon.com/dp/B08846SWQP

**SELLING PRINTS continuously.**
http://www.amazon.com/dp/B08846SWQW

**ART SCHOOL from teaching.**
http://www.amazon.com/dp/B08849FV59

**COPYRIGHT is easy money.**
http://www.amazon.com/dp/B0892HWYTV


**TAKE THE PLUNGE and Consider a Gallery.**
http://www.amazon.com/dp/B0874JF964
Hardback
http://www.amazon.com/dp/B09GQRB34T

# NOT NOW:

**Perhaps one of these books could interest you then?**

**What about your own memories?**
**YOU** could publish them – like I did!
http://www.amazon.com/dp/B087DWKPTP

**A simple way to start developing creativity.**
If you are a parent, teacher or someone who meets a group regularly?
http://www.amazon.com/dp/B088T1KFQZ

**The way most people start to become an artist!**
http://www.amazon.com/dp/B088Y1DPL6

**About some more of my memories.**
http://www.amazon.com/dp/B088Y4RPL9

## S E N D   T O :

**Know anyone interested in chocolate recipes?**
**Send them a link then.**
http://www.amazon.com/dp/B0882HK9Q9


**Know anyone interested in THIS book?**
http://www.amazon.com/dp/B0884D9TBP

www.ingramcontent.com/pod-product-compliance
Lightning Source LLC
Chambersburg PA
CBHW020605220526
45463CB00006B/2453